In This Hour

Poems
Sandra Sloss Giedeman

Green Tara Press
2014

Green Tara Press
Los Angeles, CA
www.greentarapress.com

ISBN 978-0-9898305-5-3 Paperback
978-0-9898305-6-0 Electronic Book Text

First Printing, 2014

Cover photo by Sandra Giedeman
Cover and interior design by
Lilly Penhall, Interstellar Graphics
www.interstellargraphics.com

Sandy Giedeman is a modern master of imagery and mood. Her eloquent, perceptive poetry transports you to places you wish you've been and makes you feel the human experience on a deeper emotional level. I love her work. To read it is to become more alive and more aware.

— David Ferrell
author of *Screwball* (HarperCollins Publishers) and
Pulitzer Prize-winning journalist at the Los Angeles Times

Sandra Giedeman's poetry takes the reader to a mid-summer afternoon in the Midwest or an evening along the concrete riverbed of Los Angeles. There it encourages one to pause, consider, reflect. One leaves the page refreshed and wiser.

— Jean Hastings Ardell
Breaking into Baseball: Women and the National Pastime
Southern Illinois University Press, 2005

Each word of these elegant, powerful poems falls as a tear, a smile, a heartache, and above all, love and beauty, whether Giedeman is describing a naked tree, her father's worn face, or memories of growing up in an America that struggled to sustain itself. Few poets can evoke the emotions as instantly and with such deep purity as those written here.

— Jill Amadio
Journalist and award-winning author of *Digging Too Deep*

Grateful acknowledgment is made to the editors of the following journals and anthologies where certain of these poems, sometimes in earlier versions, first appeared:

Poetry: "Eyes"
Mudfish: "10 p.m. Los Angeles"
Paris/Atlantic, American University of Paris: "On Reading Lorca"
Fiera Lingua, Italy: "Indian Summer"
Bellevue Literary Review, NYU School of Medicine: "Spring at the Coronado Hotel"
Crab Lines Off the Pier, UK Anthology: "Summer of '67"
Assisi, St. Francis College: "Autumn Flight"
Shaking Like a Mountain: "Peacock Alley"
Two Hawks Quarterly: "Son of a Shaman," "Los Angeles Basin"
Off-Channel: "Desert Angel"
Connecticut River Review: "L. A. Art Class"
Clapboard House: "Wilfred"
California Poetry Quarterly: "Ensenada Bufadora," "Venice Beach," "Baja Beach"
About Place: "Gray Iron"
Fried Chicken and Coffee: "Wilfred"
Pearl: "Visit to a California Monastery"
Nob Hill Pen Women's Poetry: "Two-Tone Ford Victoria"
Letters to Angel City Anthology: "Dark Horse"
Salem College Poetry Competition: "Sisters," "Santa Barbara"
TimesTimes3: "Route 66"
Houseboat: "Visit to California Monastery," "Ensenada Bufadora," "Desert Angel," "On Reading Lorca"

Table of Contents

for John and Edie

In This Hour

The golden hour, sometimes called the "magic hour" is the last hour of light before sunset. At this time the sun produces a diffused light that is not found at any other time. The golden hour occurs very close to the blue hour and both lights are heavily sought after by photographers because the light quality is nearly impossible to replicate at any other time. The golden hour is when the light creates a gold cast to the landscape.

Visit to a California Monastery

The wild artichokes are dry with whiskers
and faces bent like ancient ancestors
of sunflowers. Olive trees, flower-tipped
cacti, rusty barbed wire fence.

I hear the birds as clearly
as I once did in the Ozarks.

The monk is old, with blue eyes unseemingly
young. No clouds today, just open sky, oak
savannahs, silence broken by the thunder of
an F18 training jet from Miramar.

If I sit long enough I think the ache will
leave my bones. My shoulders will unlock,
my jaw unclench. There's the dull tap of a
woodpecker working one of the sycamores.
The wild rude call of a jay.

A row of million dollar houses sit atop
a ridgeline visible behind a solitary Century
plant, its flowers turned to brown. The sun rolls
in waves on my back and the day is full of space.

I think how the monk's eyes are young, but this
canyon is old—once owned by coyotes, hawks,
mountain lions, unseen rattlesnakes; recluses among
the rocks and sage on this brilliant day.

Resolution

Small orange flame, smell of Fall
leaves burning—things I no longer want

ingratitude
procrastination

Days of fog and small chores
staying ahead of dust and memories.

Regrets. The word reminds me of
an old song, *Regrets, I've had a few...*
Sinatra. Wish I could remember the lyrics.

A gray cat sits intensely focused
on something unseen on the other side
of the door.

Matins

This is Zaca Lake where
mockingbirds call curfew at
dusk, their evening litany.

Raucous crows shriek across
trees, cackling like drunks
before they settle, wings
tucked in for the night.

Just after sunset bats
fly blindly at eye level
across our path, one
finally flattening itself
against the inside wall of
our cabin.

A grey squirrel atop a tree stump
calls taps to his minions.

Sounds give way to frogs
crickets, far-off coyote calls and
a sky lit by the Orionids.

At dawn jays awaken us
noisily snatching
peanuts we laid in a row
on the fence.

The night creatures have retreated.
The bat gone now from the wall
washed with morning sun shining
through the lace of spider work.

Peacock Alley

On a back street in St. Louis near
the banks of the Mississippi where
the Admiral riverboat paddle wheeler
cruised the muddy water on summer nights.
Peacock Alley in Gaslight Square.

The laughing boy and I loved jazz and being
the only white kids at the hidden club
where we listened to Miles Davis
play "All of You" and learned something
about music, about grace and heartbreak.

I sat with the laughing boy, drank rum and coke.
He was one of those who peak early.
Collar turned up, hair slicked. He wore
pegged pants and a faded jacket. Smoked Camels
and squinted through clouds of smoke.
The charm later turned to a potbelly I heard
but God! that night, that smile—all gums and
eager.

Fourth of July, 1950

I'm six, holding a burnt sparkler.
My sister makes crazy eights
until hers dies too. Wilson Park,
weeping willows, time to go home.

Smell of gunpowder lingering from
fireworks. It is dark walking through
the trees. Father says the night landscape
reminds him of France, a World War II
battle when he was an infantry foot soldier.

Two of my brothers are not
yet born and now long dead.

That night stuck like no others. Was it
the shadowy trees? The smell of black
powder that triggered Father's memories?
I remember the now-spent wand of ashes.
Delicate as smoke, toppling into nothing.
The crunch of leaves underfoot. The blue
chlorine smell of the night swimming pool.
That Midwest summer of heat waves and
polio, cherry bombs and firecrackers.

Gray Iron

Long gone Massey Dairy its
overgrown fountain out front where
sluggish carp once floated in algae.

Streets deserted, eerie, absent of sound.
Scaffolds of indifference
buildings collapsed or paved over
left to winter and wind.

Midwest mill town bounded by rivers
the Mississippi, Ohio, Wabash.

I remember something alive here.
Stockyards, blood and shit of the animals
stench of terror, sensing their own impending
death. Smokestack spewing its sulphurous
smell. Steel mill with its own language;
blast furnace, hod carrier, slag
millwright, pig iron, skelp.

Mother was a swan in a junkyard here.
Father remote and wounded, put away
his war medals to feed us, send us to
Catholic school. Echoes of horn blasts
at noon shift change, fire-embered
floors and the heat of Hell.

Smell of cabbage stewing, sleet, snow
gray and black landscape of slush and ice
rust everywhere. It all disappeared so slowly
as to be hardly noticeable. What is left behind?
All that is unyielding, unforgiving, hard.

A River Town

Has air that carries the nature of the river
along where levees and riverboats move
slowly, leave elegant ripples of wake.
Rough, hard-working barges roll alongside.

And the bridges arching over the Mississippi;
works of art, old, fraught with rust, ironwork
delicate enough to rival that of the Eiffel Tower.
The French Soulard market at the riverfront.

Home of blues musicians, jazz, gamblers
fried catfish, gangsters, dance halls. A St. Louis
that glowed in the nights of the '20s, '30s, '40s.

It's all gone now, but on summer nights
you can feel the memory of it in the air.
I'm a like a fishmonger who can never
wash away the smell of a place.

Two-Tone Ford Victoria

Father had a knack, a special gift
for buying cars that immediately
became obsolete, the shiny
green Hudson Hornet
the Henry J, the black Packard
that looked like a mob car.
The Mercury, big heavy thing
with windows like gun turrets.
A tank. An upside-down bathtub.

He loved his cars and when he was young
he jazzed them up with special mud flaps.
The last one I remember was the red Cadillac
a '59, with jutting tail fins that resembled
weapons mounted on the rear.

He always bought what he called Detroit Iron.
Wasn't thrilled with my first car, an MG1600.
Would have preferred for me to buy the
two-tone green and white Ford Victoria
with chrome strips running along the side.

He loved his cars as much as he loved
Johnny Cash and Hank Williams. I thought
that music maudlin, but years later when
country music came into vogue, I surprised
myself when I knew all the lyrics to "Orange
Blossom Special" and "Your Cheatin' Heart."

June Gloom

June is a beach that smells of red tide
water listlessly lapping at the sand
a squadron of seagulls scanning the horizon
a marine layer
birds the color of fog.

It will burn off, is the chant
hoping for sun, rationalizing weather
with our clichés, as we say about August
at least it's a dry heat.

We are summer in winter
aging white-bearded surfers
smell of sun block. Sun slipping into
the Pacific, a barely noticed pink disc.

Then July with its white sun, everything
burned into high relief. Fat lizards scattering
around my front door.

It is hard to mark the passage of time for
a transplant from elsewhere. Where are the
snowsuits that reek of cedar and mothballs?
The rubber galoshes, mittens, earmuffs
beaver collars on winter coats?

Here's how summer arrives; the mockingbird
returns to sit atop the same telephone pole.
He sings me awake and asleep while
the Monkey's Paw in the garden sends up its
spindly mustard flowers to reach for the sun.

Los Angeles Basin

The Santa Ana rolls like a hell wheel across
mountains, blows smog out to the Pacific.
Sunset is toxic copper, metallic. Strange
how poisoned air is luminous. Wind and light
drug me. Everything I see has equal weight.

Small-shouldered oil derricks pump near a concrete
gorge, a trickle of water known as the Los Angeles River
courtesy of the Flood Control District. A white egret
poses, a paper cutout against the gray mud of the river.

Palm fronds, bougainvillea, adobe cottages
power lines. I look at the sky, remember that
I heard a man say, "California is heartbreaking.
It tries to be Paradise, but it's broken."

The Santa Ana dies and a countervailing wind
picks up, whistles past car windows, the 405, the 15,
Downey, Hawaiian Gardens, Riverside, on out to
the desert to be caught and churned in Coachella Valley
windmills spinning like toys on the sands of the Mojave.

The Best Sunset Is Always the Last

Santa Ana, mistral, papagayo; rogue winds
that whistle, whirl. Create a light so bright it
renders the sand at Joshua Tree a blinding white.
Outlaw winds that burnish canyons; ripple light
in a French meadow.

I study the Vermeer woman at a window; soft
morning light on her face, light falling across
folds of fabric, into shadows. Artists capture
fire, freeze a blaze, paint an inferno, capture a
17th Century profile, a fleeting sunrise,
the frail ghost of dawn.

Today, light like clover honey washes the walls.
Romeo and Juliet shared those walls, those colors.
Light that softened Vermeer's women; drove
Van Gogh to paint swirls of gold sky, his brush
heavy with pigments he mixed himself. Light
is time that moves and changes with the wind.
Artists paint time.

Midnight in San Clemente

A long freight train
wends through town on tracks
at the water's edge, whistle blowing.

I could be anywhere else—
a brick railroad flat
in a steel mill town, a riverboat
on the brown Mississippi, a lonely
farm in the Ozark hollows or that
small Midwestern apartment, his last
where my father sat alone
tobacco-stained and gray.

I know that whistle—
plaintive
pervasive
blowing across the land.

Saturday in Santa Monica

Cilantro, olive oil, Ray Bans
skinny people dressed in black.

Want your veggie burger on
focaccia?
Soy latte, non-fat?
Rosti Restaurant, Montana Avenue.
I've had four hours of sleep
and the restaurant is noisy
clanging pots, blondes
on cell phones. Yoga gear.
Range Rovers parked outside.

The guy at the table near me is
chewing with his mouth open.
He would have made my Dad proud.

The waitress points
"Don't forget to eat
your biscotti," and this place
feels like a movie set.

Maybe I'll loosen up
write something good if I borrow
the green Crayola from the little girl
at the next table. Write with that.
See what comes.

Some days I feel like that
bananafish Seymour talked about.

(...)

The little girl with the green
crayon wears black nail polish
and the poster on the wall
says *Bozon Verduraz* and I
don't know what that means.

Someone translate, please?

Light

One day I looked out the window
and saw light as if for the first time
the permeable quality of it and its effect.

Radiant light of California, midday July
phosphorescent along the shore.

Filtered light at Big Sur where I saw
what dappled means, the dance
of sun and redwoods.

This remembering. The context of scenes—
dust-moted light in St. Joseph's late afternoon
waiting for my turn in the confessional.

Early morning light coming in slabs through east
facing windows. Steel-gray light in the fifth grade
classroom. Shadowy autumn light just before dark
walking home through dry puddles of red leaves.

Then, in California, listening to conversations
about the light in Northern California versus
Southern California and how it differs for artists.

Natural light that the magazine photographer
needed, he said, as we watched it fade fast.

People on the pier at sunset. A religious rite
the way they gather to watch the dying of the
light, then turn and scatter slowly.

I'm losing the light, my brother said. What
he always said when the depression struck.

Hotel Bohemé

The scent of sea air and fish, of spices
wafting from a Sutter Street café. At
night, the near-to-decay smell of red tide.
A shop on Columbus where a man rolls
truffles in clouds of chocolate dust. The
street outside a sea of black umbrellas.

Fog hill of ship horns, the cry of gulls.
People wrapped in long coats and scarves.
Midnight in North Beach. A vacant lot wet with

rain reflects blinking neon. People step out
of limos, oblivious laughter drifts up. The
proprietor of the hotel pours sherry, tells me,
"Allen Ginsberg slept here." Oh yes, poet with
the heart of a bleeding bomb. A raindrop rolls
down the window collecting others on its way.

Indian Summer

Trees my husband insists
on calling deciduous turn to fire.
Fall means another year to stand
at a barn in Julian and heft blood red
Jonathans, Winesaps, scarlet and tart.
Later I'll peel the dark skins away
in one long spiral, naked flesh
quickly turning brown.

I move past bins mounded with dried
corn, squash, gourds, pumpkins, ripe
but not summer ripe, these are older,
seasoned. I trace curves and run my fingers
over their bumpy skins. Autumn yellow
orange, bumpy as fifty Octobers. Cloves
coriander, cinnamon.

We drive the mountain road home.
"There's an ancient landslide," he says
pointing at a rocky cliff. A tumble
of harvest spills on the back seat.
We point out things to one another.
A brilliant red tree glimpsed
here, wild artichokes there.
An argument hangs in the bright air.
In October you can change your life.

Venice Beach, California

I took my Indiana cousin to
Venice Beach where we milled
with tattooed gangbangers
rottweilers on leashes
cholos with gorgeous faces.
Rap music. Chimichangas
bubbling in lard mixed with
the smell of ocean salt.
Jamaican tin drummers
in a trance of concentration.

My cousin whispered, "look at that guy."
He pointed at a man who had moussed
his hair into devil horns, dyed them red
and scored women from 1 to 10
as they roller-skated by in bikinis.

Muscle Beach weightlifters.
"Steroid mutants," my cousin muttered.

We looked down perpendicular streets
a different universe from the beach
a block away. Streets named Wavecrest
and Navy. Rows of houses with overgrown
shrubs and sunny second story windows on
a late afternoon in November.

Porches, frame houses. Hydrangeas.
"This looks like home," my cousin said, suddenly
comfortable. We had walked into an Edward Hopper

painting. Sun struck the facades at tangents so pleasing
that we stared until it all changed to something
pedestrian, commonplace, shabby, serviceable.
As if all who moved here from Ohio, Indiana, Missouri
carried our Main Streets with us.

Summer of '67

Sky's orange shadows lunging
lonely as water crushing mown fields
lacewings shuttling, smell of roses.

Over too soon. We did not know
what was to happen next.

Stars to all of us who looked up.
Sin and constellations.
Wine for those we could forgive.

Life was not denial, nor disbelief.
We were fig leaves in the wind.
Flowers friendly to the bees.

We invented flame but then felt the dark
coming in sun's heat to melt the fields.

We didn't see the rising darkness
complete and gutted like candles.

Sisters

You will relent like you always do
dial her number and let it ring and ring
you will wonder where she could be and she'll
tell you later that afternoon when she calls back
that she can only get a signal on her cell phone
when she puts it on the fence outside.

She'll tell you that she's in Kentucky
where she's decided to move with Mike.
You will want to say, why do you want to bury
yourself in the backwoods but you don't
knowing she won't speak to you again if you do.

You will listen to her high on her two-week isolation
telling you again how there's no signal for her phone
how there are no people there to interrupt or annoy
her by stopping her to talk at Wal-Mart or ask about
the drug addict her oldest son is involved with.

You will listen, then hang up feeling anxious
and you're not sure why. You will ponder this and
decide it has to do with age and the thought that
your sister has chosen her place to die.

You'll think about how she used to be
and how she's changed and you've changed
and how you're growing farther and farther apart.
She'll tell you she'll send pictures of the farm
and you'll say great knowing she never will.

Ensenada Bufadora

I wanted to buy the paper maché devil
in a red chair that day, remember?
Hand painted pink skin and rouged cheeks
tiny horns poking through shiny black hair.
I liked that. Satan in an armchair.
And the mud fetish doll with the
crown of thorns and tiny nails
encircling the head.

You chose a skeleton in a sombrero
at a stand festooned with blue piñatas
near the bufadora. Handed it to me.

We saw dolphins and drank Coronas.
Talked about nothing on this stray weekend
probably our last together. We
watched a rat dart across the patio
at a beach restaurant with fruit
of a color too brilliant to eat.
The place thick with bougainvillea
dripping purple against the stucco
where bats buzzed in flurries of black
dodging the falling night.

On Reading Lorca

To drown in green: an abrupt end some would say
but to me it would be a bath in lichen, mossy and soft
rolling in gray green waves of eucalyptus leaves.

I would cover myself in palm fronds, cool undersides
against my bare legs. Olive-colored pools floating over
loamy soil, sea foam waves lapping at my sand-covered feet

Washing away khaki dust. Poison green, hemlock green
shady glens, arbors, vines curling and twisting up
cliffs of jade and malachite.

I'd wrap myself in the green blanket of my body.
Gaze through algae eyes. Zampoã music carried on
wind high above mountains rising from the ocean floor
reaching to stab the swirling emerald sky.

Ode to Piped-In Music

I'm on hold to have a question
answered. I've listened to
three cyber-robot messages
and haven't connected with a human.
Some Donna Summer comes on.
Good, I can reminisce about the '70s.

Oh, the dentist's chair? I'm Novocain numbed
and over the hum of the drill, "Feelings," one
of the all-time drippiest songs plays. And yet, the
drawn-out, "feelings, oh, oh, oh, feelings,"
seems appropriate now, when I can't feel.

Then, there's the elevator at Saks. The muzak
all the way up to the third floor is The Clash,
"Should I Stay or Should I Go" played by 101 Strings.
I look on it philosophically. Everything
gets rolled into the mainstream eventually.

The best piped-in music, really, by far, is
the Union 76 Station in San Juan Capistrano
where the owner pipes Mozart and Brahms
out to the pumps. I feel noble as I fill up
with regular every week.

Last time there was a bit of a problem
when the kid at the next pump played rap
so loud on his sound system that his Chevy
appeared to vibrate along with the bass.

The Pizza Kitchen has it all planned out.
They blast some indefinable music genre—
loud and tinny. Wonderful way for the
management to get a rapid turnover at the tables.

I see us all carried along on waves of sound
chosen by people we don't know and will never see.

My husband made his selection for his funeral.
He wants Van Morrison's "Real Real Gone"
played. I haven't chosen my music yet. Maybe
I'll be a maverick and have silence.

Southern Illinois Summer

July chlorine of the swimming
pool, nothing but time
in the wet heat of summer.

Fireworks explode with muffled
thuds white chrysanthemum bloom.
July chlorine of the swimming pool.

Sugary Nehi orange, melting ice cream
low whispers of picnickers watching
in the wet heat of summer.

Sundresses glow like cotton candy
blue water and calls of children
July chlorine of the swimming pool.

The fourth of July before everyone
hopped the train to California
in the wet heat of summer.

Weeping willows at Wilson Park
sparklers burn to wands of ashes.
July chlorine of the swimming pool
in the wet heat of summer.

Spring at the Coronado Hotel

We watch the gardener arc a hose
carelessly washing away the work
of mud sparrows, hornets and wasps.
Nests studded with white eggs
in the intricate catacombs they constructed
under the eaves of the hotel.
A single red flower sways near our table.
My mother planted a crooked row
of tulips that color
from the corner of our house to the street
when we all still spoke to one another.
When we thought death happened to old people
not to our brother that beautiful boy
with the strawberry blond hair and deep voice
who cried easily. Delicate collarbones
alabaster freckled skin.
My husband and I eat a bright salad
under an umbrella.
A hummingbird is close.
I hear the whir of his wings
as he dives, then hovers over my head.

People in the Sun

(Painting by Edward Hopper)

To swim in the height of summer
Midwest lake stung with lightning bolts.
Watch a young soldier pitch forward
in a dead faint at a Memorial Day celebration.

A brother disappear down steps
on a sunny afternoon.
A mother board her flight at LAX
with one last turn to wave goodbye.

A father in the street receding
in a rearview as I drive away.
A canopy of black umbrellas,
on a gray day at Union Square.

A turtle soup celebration in deep woods
uncles cooking the creatures in a cauldron
while the roiling clack buzz of grasshoppers
seems to come from inside my head.

A small town in the '50s where
I return in thoughts, but not in dreams.
Certain music comes to mind
bluegrass, church organs, staticky radio.

Tom Waits, Tom Waits. I'm listening to you
sing that music can tell us terrible things
your words echoing through circus instruments.

I've driven perfectly and safely for miles
and I realize I don't know where I've been.

Look What's Become of Me

The watches and clocks stopped.
I never bothered to wind them.
Like a wooden top spinning
on a cold stone porch
in an old four-family flat
finally falling still.

A wooden Regulator with gongs
glass and brass
like the halos on saints.
The hands stopped at 6:20
Greenwich Mean Time
Daylight Savings time.

"Come in, come in," mother called
"it's getting dark." I ran
barefoot and the rain was warm.
Relative time like Einstein and his theory
Time is a snake's discarded skin
a ball of string you call your life.

Summer rain plops dusty drops
washes away the chalk hopscotch.

Now, I always check my watch.
"Am I keeping you?" he asked.
No, no. Summer is over
Get on with it, I want to say.

No more time for blue wooden benches
at the old outdoor movie theater. Orange
soda and popcorn and those summer nights.

Wilfred

My uncle was proud of his blue tick hounds
his sixty acres of hills, hollows, creeks filled
with copperheads and cottonmouths;
nights utterly still except when a smell or sound
riled the hounds from their sleep
to bay like old mourners.

He read aloud Sunday mornings
from the Book of Job in a nasal voice
of hating the night and waiting for day
only to find in the day that one wished for night
about how we are here for a flicker of time
then reflected in no one's eye.

My aunt had the custom of Ozark people of keeping
framed photographs of dead relatives in their coffins.
When my uncle died she got rid of his hounds, his
jews harp, said she was through with men
and their ways, but she kept his death photo displayed
on a lace doily in her living room.

Dark Horse

Horses that glisten like polished mahogany.
Topiary, Art Deco buildings, shadowy stalls
pervasive odor of manure, Santa Anita with
handsome little jockeys from Panama and
60-something waitresses who whisper sure-bets.

A guy like someone from the Maltese Falcon
walks past. "Hey Smoke," his friends call. He is
perfectly groomed with slicked hair, a yellow scarf
around his neck, shoes split open at the seams.

The grandstand roars as a dead last longshot pulls ahead
the jockey's whip flashing a tempo on its flanks. "People
love underdogs. It's human nature," my father always said.
"Silky Sullivan was the famous come-from-behinder.
He'd be so far out of the picture he wasn't even part of
the announcer's call and then, last minute there he was
passing every horse like they was standin' still."

To him, people were either winners or losers, and "only
the winner goes to dinner." He taught me to read the form;
the esoteric language of furlongs, fractions, sires, dams,
game efforts, mudders, claimers. Years ago he asked
me to scatter his ashes across the finishing line.
When I am lonely I go to the track.

Father

Sen-Sen, the hard licorice candy that
covers the smell of tobacco or Jack Daniels.
Old Spice. Vitalis sprinkled
like holy water on his hair, parted on
the left, fresh comb marks
leaving a trail. A star sapphire ring
on his pinkie. Feet too small for
his plump body. Purple Heart, Bronze
Stars pinned to his lapel. Someone
wound a rosary around his fingers.
He would have hated that.

Santa Barbara

A carp breaks the lake's surface
the sound of crickets his chorus.
A great horned owl glides above
an old man who fills mason jars with
what he calls sacred mud of the healing lake.

In the lobby of faded sun, I pass row after row
of pinned butterflies under glass
Anise Swallowtail
Mournful Duskywing
Cabbage White
Memento Mori of this old hotel, long-gone guests
days of green and summer's
sulphurous heat bursting cocoons.

Fragile speckled wings that someone felt
the need to pin down.
You're awake as a child until they teach you
the names of things.

Point

Don't point. An early rule from a parent
like, don't talk politics or religion. Don't point.

On the point, where the lighthouse rotated
its warning beacon to warn ships away.

The whole point of this experiment, conversation
event is to resolve, come to a conclusion.

I run through the points. Now you make
your points, or it's all pointless.
That was a pointed comment.

After that screw-up I've lost innumerable
points with the boss, he said, hangdog.

Points of light in the night sky.
Points of firefly glow in the dusk.

He danced in pointy shoes
so pointy they curled up at the toes.

His pointy chin gave him a chiseled aspect.

In Euclidean geometry, a point is a
primitive notion.

What's the point?
The point of all this? I don't know.
I think I missed the point.

At some point we've reached the point of no return.

Acres of Books

The place was so dusty I needed to be hosed
down when I left. It was near the beach
in a seedy part of town with fly-specked windows
and a map display that hadn't been changed in forever.

I miss that bookstore in Long Beach
where I sometimes found cheaply priced
first editions. Where, one day, a black
wreath hung on the wall.
"Our fifty-year employee passed away,"
the clerk said.

I liked to browse the shelves for arcane titles
"The Adventures of Baron Munchausen"
Victorian poetry, old science fiction
Raymond Chandler, essays, biographies.

Mementos people had tucked between pages;
an unfinished love letter, dated 1960, from
Sylvia to Mark, Venice, California.
Pressed flowers that fluttered from pages.
Books filled with doodles, opinions penciled in.

The last time I was there I saw Ray Bradbury
foraging through the stacks. A hulking presence, he
caught me looking at him, smiled, and said, "Research."
Acres of Books, gone away like so many temples to books.

Son of a Shaman

He's Peruvian, the son of a shaman. "Come see my painting," he'd said. "Stand close to the glass." What appeared solid from a distance was actually a mass of intertwined symbols close up, sacred symbols.

He shows me his "Queen of Rods" painting. Nine orange cups and green fish vibrate through cut glass windows in what appears to be late afternoon sun. There's a strange flower with green leaves too-large overwhelming the gray flower. I peer at the painting and see a woman's pale face, drained, weary. Plants in the background appear green and strong, with stems like poles, stamens like innards. The woman's neck and arms are covered. She's outshone by purple dahlias surrounding her. The only colorless thing in this painting is her face. It's been borrowed—her color—and given to the flowers. A mutated sunflower steals color from her eyes. Thick auburn hair waves and twists. The Queen of Rods wears a crown. There are thorns everywhere, but not on her crown. She's flat as an icon, and I can't read her expression. I can only guess. She's the Queen of Secondary Colors.

"I see hummingbirds in there," I said. "Yes," he said. "In the Amazon, we call them the bringers of fire. In Mexico, they are a darker symbol of the underworld." His art is painted on glass. "I didn't work for a couple of years," he said. We all knew about his depression. Not even the Ayahuasca trips to South America had helped. His friend had said, "Maybe you'll talk to him. You're a poet. He respects that. His brother is a poet."

Autumn Flight

Stella Star, Belinda Blue, Helena,
Pandora; climbing roses that cling to
the doorframe in a garden gone to seed.
Puff a dandelion and ghostly slivers fly.

Mother's red Chow Simon strains at his
leash when I walk him today. He bares a
Buddha dog smile at me—
black gums and tongue.

I choose the green dress to bury her in.
Her shroud. Archaic word. Archaic as Ozark
cemeteries. She took death photos of her
loved ones. She would pull out the picture
of dad in his coffin. "Handsome, wasn't he?"

Today I toss out white geraniums someone
has sent. She hated geraniums. "Put geraniums
on my grave and I'll come back to haunt you."

Calvary Cemetery. We walk past the graves
of Saggy who owned the Skelly gas station.
Cleta who played the church organ.
Doc Hamm who swabbed our sore throats.
Aunts, uncles, brothers.

Raucous geese pass in a ragged V
and are gone.

Artists of the Freeway

Fat letters crowd together, swoops of color
sprayed so high above traffic lanes the
tagger has to be adept at walking
tightropes.

Each tagger with his distinctive style
that becomes familiar after my fourth drive
past the School of Performing Arts, Cathedral
of Our Lady of the Angels, the Music Center.

Is the loopy graffiti along the 101 a message
in a language too esoteric for me? Hieroglyphics
painted by night squads in code only street
gangs understand. We own this city, they

are saying—bougainvillea on chain-link
fences, red-tail hawks perched on phone poles,
bare walls that we fill with incantations
palm trees cracking through concrete. All of it.

Ernie 31, SF Brothers, Boyle Heights Chuey
spell it out for us in word, color, image
portraits, obscure warnings. Los Angeles
sacred city, underworld of urban art.

Donald, Laurel Canyon 1997

He showed me his perfume collection.
This one is for you, he said, handing me
a blown-glass bottle filled with a French
perfume of tuberose and gardenia.
He sprayed me with a patchouli scent
so strong it stayed with me all day.

I like this one, he said, reminds me
of incense at Sunday Mass.
I got another chance at life and
I won't blow it this time. The drugs
are working. His Mississippi drawl
his delicate head, flesh drawn tight.

You look better this week, I said.

His hand fluttered, weighed down by
the diamond ring he called Baby Liz.
His bedroom was fit for a young prince.
Books tumbled about in the living room
where he taught poetry, schooling us in the
fine points of Plath, Eliot, sestinas, villanelles.

I saw him one last time before he died at 38.
He wore a black silk kimono open to the waist
his hair slicked back, debonair as Valentino.
Late summer heat wafted through windows
brushed with late summer roses and peonies.

Baja Beach

A steady slosh of waves
render the ocean's secrets.
A dead bird rocked by the waves
in a last lullaby, bits of shells
detritus drifting
riding high tide.

The Pacific whispers
throwing ropes of seaweed
entrails of the newly dead
onto the sand. Buzzing flies
hover, a lone seagull
picks among slippery vines
darts and retreats.

This Mexican beach is a dark dream
where midnight fireworks flare
explosions are muffled, colors
dimmed by distance.

Night holds my hand, running
with wounded feet toward
the last vapors of the moon
leached of color stealing its
light from the sun. I watch
the pale lizard of morning
slither across the horizon.

I close my eyes and an intricate
amoeba floats into view
followed by a small creature
that lazily cartwheels across
my field of vision.

Eyes

We see gray vistas
bleeding heart of pomegranate
lightning bolts on a lake.
Our eyes focusing, remembering
leaving no record.
A solitary camera
a consciousness that dies.
I want to gaze through my
Great-grandmother's eyes.
To see what she saw
on her last trip out of Scotland.
To be a voyeur
in a dingy second-hand shop.
A basket of forgotten photos.
A scruffy sheaf of black and whites.
Greedy for frozen memories
I fan the scallop edged pictures.
A man with a cane and a monocle.
A woman leaning on the fender of a roadster.
Memories soaked like rum in a sponge cake.
Three dustbowl Okies
Rincon Camp 1932 penciled on the back.
One of them holds a long-forgotten infant.
A straw-hatted man sitting on a dune.
Coal eyes, wet eyes, weary seen everything eyes.
Skin stretched over bones, turning to folds.
Then light pure light
from the eyes staring out.
I want to know the last thing my mother saw.

Mojave Landscape

Furnace Creek, Death Valley
29 Palms, Joshua Tree, Needles.
This desert strewn with creosote
crucifixion thorns, ocotillo
sinuous roots of greasewood
growing below sand and dust.

Alluvial fans, diatomaceous
earth, scarred as the moon
filled with serpents
tiny monsters, webbed feet
horned lizard, gecko, iguana.

Creatures of claws, fangs
forked tongues, unblinking eyes
curved tails spewing venom
muted tambourine of a rattlesnake
nearby. Enter at your own risk
reads a bullet-pocked sign.

The horizon shimmers in heat
ripples like imaginary waves.
Buzzards float high in a lazy circle.
Something died out here.
It lies facing the sky
offers up its bead of a heart
to vultures descending
in a slow, practiced spiral.

Ten p.m. Los Angeles

Ten p.m. is silence in a Hollywood Hills house
with hardwood floors and a husband who doesn't speak.
Is watching a meteor shower at a deserted beach in Baja.
Is a brother that calls from jail in tears to ask for bail
and I say no, not knowing he'll be dead in a month.
A walk past houses with security systems
that turn on lights as I pass.

Ten p.m. is static on AM radio and a psychologist
with a voice like silk pajamas.
Is the time I turn away from my husband
because I stopped loving him a year ago
and I don't know what to do about it.
Is the time I want to run from the house
but I don't know where.
When I don't want to hear the phone ring
because it can only be bad news.
I leave a Hollywood apartment
at Sunset and Mariposa that resembles
a Day of the Locust set. I am on the street looking up
at the Griffith Park Observatory
that reminds me of James Dean and Natalie Wood
and being young.
I hurry when I see a black car
idling at the curb, lights off, engine running.

Ten p.m. is when I see
the blind woman tapping a cane to her bus stop.
She is braver than I am.
I speed to the Hollywood freeway.

(...)

Ten p.m. is when I sit with my hands on my knees
and stare at the blinds on my window
watching them ripple and wave like a black asphalt road
in the heat of a long-ago Midwestern day.
Why did I leave? I remember what I know
about particle physics and wonder
if my eyes are playing tricks
or if the blinds are really moving
all the molecules spinning.
Small organisms float before my eyes.
Ten p.m. is when I think I could go mad in L.A.
with a birdfeeder and a barbecue outside my window.
I wasn't always like this. One thing I have learned.
Everything in life is a metaphor for everything else.

December

A sharp-shinned hawk atop my fence
stonily eyeing the doves and finches
at the feeder.

Red cliffs at Zion at sunset on
a rainy day, a young man who sells
me opal earrings, for a clean look
he says at the deserted gem shop.

Banks of California brown pelicans
whitecaps on the gray Pacific.

Three Italian Greyhounds yesterday
prancing with their owner like reindeer.

Rows of blood oranges and Winesap
apples tumbled artfully on the cart
at the farmers' market.

Four o'clock sun through my stained
glass windows taken from the closed-down
church in Colorado.

Orangewood stacked in the fireplace.

The tiny Christmas tree blinking
in a window in the surf ghetto
in our neighborhood.

(...)

Cluster of people on a park
bench who looked as if they've
been posed by an artist.

The neighbor's house bedecked with
strands of Christmas lights, red and green
that he strung around his roof and windows.

Desert Angel

I no longer believe in
the angel with flimsy wings
who loitered, then finally flew
away from a stale motel
at the edge of 29 Palms
up to the sky over Joshua Tree
leaving my brother to night sweats
mother nightmares, and thirteen rounds
from a semi-automatic in the overeager
hands of Officer Christian.

Angel with a face contrived of dry winds
that lost my brother's voice across
crackling telephone wires
interstates, gas stations army bases
midnight freight trains
moving through the Mojave.

You could never see him, even
when your angel sat in front of you
on the San Diego bus you didn't
recognize him, you too preoccupied
with your bled out bomb of a heart.
Your angel got off at the stop before yours
and pressed his face against your window
but mistaking him for a panhandler
and anxious to move on
you brushed him away.

Reverie

At this age everything reminds me
of something else. Green tea leaves
in the bottom of the cup remind me
of grandmother. Homemade chocolate
cake with a cup of sour milk poured
into the batter, of mother.
Tall glasses of iced tea with lemon slices
on the rims, Aunt Lucille.

Maraschino cherries over vanilla ice cream,
father. Pecans remind me of the blue willow
plate a neighbor kept filled for the squirrels
on the sun porch of her house where I read *Lady
Chatterley's Lover* the summer I was sixteen.

Grandmother lived in Chicago in a house with
twenty-foot ceilings. She'd lie across her bed
with the door open listening to opera on
her staticky radio, a wet washcloth on her
forehead to soothe the migraine. There was a
perpetually drained swimming pool in the back.

Once, when I was eight, I went to her basement
and saw dusty slot machines in a row under a blanket.
I remember thinking there was something unsavory
about them and I kept what I saw a secret. At night I
stood on a stool in her kitchen and listened to
"The Shadow" on the radio. The Shadow knew about
what evil lurks in the hearts of men.

Los Angeles Art Class

The Sawtelle Boulevard studio reeks
of turpentine, gesso, linseed oil mixed
with the smell of noodle soup
from the Japanese restaurant next door.

Silvery tubes of oil paints from Zora's
on San Vicente. Fat blobs of color—
poison green, crimson lake, phthalo.

I swipe the loaded brush across canvas
like a child going crazy with finger-paints.
"See what I can do!"

"Not so raw from the tube," the teacher
whispers over my shoulder.

I pick up the burnt umber to tone it all
down, swirl the paints until they're gray
and I see how we take colors
mix them together to make it better
and it turns to mud like family
relationships, sisters, brothers—
and it can't be undone.

Blackbirds Singing

Jacob brings his red-tailed hawk
its talons dig into the leather cuffs
on his wrist as he plucks the hood
from the bird's ancient yellow eyes.

We watch it swoop and soar
sun catching the rust of its tail.

Long-lived black-necked cranes
circle over a monastery in Bhutan
with a lonely clamor. They float
to ground and dance before settling.

A flock of Canadian geese
approach and pass, the sound
a deep gorge of sorrow.

Heavy-breasted doves strut on my balcony.
Turkey buzzards on a two-lane
highway crowd at a road kill.

The woman in the synagogue whispers
to her dead father for a long time as if
singing quietly to an infant to comfort.
A girl sitting straight allows one sob to escape.

Funeral of a 20-Year-Old Soldier

I don't want to see a slow cortege
moving along El Camino Real
to the San Clemente mortuary—helicopters
cops, bikers, old vets, young Marines who
lift the young soldier's casket from a white
hearse as if they'd done this forever.

I don't want to sleep in the storm.
I don't want guns aimed at the desert.
I don't want a cold night moon.
I don't want windy sand dunes.

I want a bloody pomegranate heart
split open under a warming sky.
I want to kiss the blood from his eyelids
comb the smoke from his hair.

Traveling Back

When I get the calls—mother, father, brother, brother
for only two of them have I cried.

I'm on the road listening to country music. Desert plants
roll across the asphalt like playful ghosts; dusty miller, sage.
Brother, desert rat, we teased you, cold and heat-seeking,
humming with sorrow. I want to watch you on a summer
St. Louis lawn eating a pomegranate, grabbing the taste of
life, reckless brother, mayfly who lives only a day; traitor
who abandons.

The road glimmers with a string of headlights, taillights.
The calls always come late and another link to the ruby
lights is driving away. I am sentenced to stay on my ride.
Music is a knife dividing time into decades, wafting out
windows, pushing through speakers, night on a highway.

I drive a road and dream. I loved you with all my breath.
And now you sleep, brother. The woman said he called from
Barstow and cried. Find your spot and sleep, dream under
relentless stars. You could never sleep; then you slept. I always
get the calls late at night. If I don't pick up, it hasn't happened.

Scenes From a Life

The smallest gesture, flickers that pass without
notice but are imprinted and who will I tell what
I've seen, who will remember with me, among the
variety of sketches I choose without knowing the
why of it. Click, change the view again and again.

Life has so few real moments the young man said
to the weeping woman in the elevator descending
to open doors. What holds? What stays? Is a primal
vision in the mind's eye so personal, that only we
can see.

Yesterday it was the old man sitting next to me in
Starbucks, humming to himself. The hum like a bee
drawing near then away. The old man struggled to
his feet and I noticed his stained pants.

Now, I look out the window and see freeways, palm
trees, California. But if I close my eyes I can see a
road winding like a ribbon through Ozark trees,
scarlet in October, and an aunt innocent as a child.
I'm a collector of pictures that tumble and turn and
I keep adding, adding like yesterday – six crows
over the Santa Ana freeway attacking the red tail
that swooped and soared trying to keep away from
their murderous beaks, sun picking up the speckled
wings. What does it mean? Does it need a reason?

Cabin on Volcon View, Julian

White-washed walls, cathedral windows
birds chirping in oaks. There's a dead
tree just outside the window, its leaves
long gone. Musical instruments are
strewn about the room, guitars, an old
accordion, a zither. A Chagall print
of a bridal couple floating in the sky
a goat playing cello beneath them.

The pioneer cemetery three hills away
is bronzed in the lilting afternoon sun.

Three women are in the cabin, quiet, not talking.
Window blinds chatter in the weak breeze
like birds at a feeder and two spiders black as ink
scurry in the sink. There's a smell of coffee
and fireplace charred from winter snow fires.
The refrigerator whirs its white noise while
the light of the sun moves across the wooden
bunkhouse walls outside.

The three women write.

Kaleidoscope

Flat landscape behind a '54 Plymouth, Kansas, 1963.
A faded Polaroid of mother, two of her sons both
dead by their thirties, standing in front of her.

A Doors song on the radio heading to L. A. I recall
Topanga Canyon, amber lights, mudslides, patchouli
and the artist I painted with into the night, for many nights.

The way my niece turns her head, reminding me so much
of my brother that it takes my breath away. My daughter's
sharp humor, her elegant loping walk, coming to meet me.

The smell of Joy, Aramis, cigarettes, that remind me of
Peacock Alley, St. Louis where I heard Miles Davis play.

The parade of dogs, cats. The black and white cat that lived
to 17, sporting a black mustache on his white face. The Italian
Greyhound who ran like the wind across a field one day.

The enormous owl on my mailbox. He doesn't fly at my
approach but swivels his stately head to take my measure.

The Joe Louis bar in East St. Louis with the glowing Wurlitzer.
The enormous Belgian workhorse on my aunt's farm that stood
patiently under the lightning struck tree so that we could
climb up on his broad back.

The older I become, the more all of these memories and smells
become long hallways I wander, or the bright moment when a
train barrels out of a tunnel on its snowy ride through Oregon.
A gift. A kaleidoscope I can turn and twist at will.

Route 66

String of pearl night cities
white headlights, ruby taillights
deserted roadside rests, main streets
giving way to rock upheavals, buttes,
white bones visible in black hills. Dark
towns called Jerome. Tumbleweeds,
high wind. A desert called Mojave.
Miles from prairies and home.

The two of us young strangers in
midnight towns glowing along Route 66.
The Mother Road, they called it.
"King of the Road," the only song
we hear on the Plymouth's scratchy radio.

Caught in the slipstream of time
driving through forgotten places
wingbeats shadowing our past.

Weight of time circling, tightening
until we feel ourselves swept along in
down slope winds. All the years,
miles, distances we traveled together.

That time was weightless. Our wings those
of a map opened and folded again and again.
Left behind on a table somewhere in Oklahoma.

About the Author

Sandra Sloss Giedeman was born in St. Louis, Missouri and grew up in Granite City, Illinois, the oldest of five children, winning the National Spelling Bee when she was twelve. In her 20's she moved to California and worked as editor of several trade and consumer magazines and owner of Upchurch-Brown Booksellers in Laguna Beach, California. Giedeman is past president of the Orange County Chapter of PEN and was on the California State University Fullerton extension writing program advisory board.

Sandra has been published in various journals and anthologies including publications in France, Italy, and the UK, and was honored to read at Shakespeare & Company in Paris with a small group of poets. She has a Pushcart Nomination and several poetry awards including the Mudfish Poetry Prize. The New Short Fiction Series in Los Angeles presented an evening of her short stories. Sandra has a grown daughter and lives in San Clemente, California with her husband.

Connect with Sandra Giedeman

Email: sgiedeman@aol.com

Facebook: www.facebook.com/sandra.giedeman

LinkedIn: http://www.linkedin.com/pub/
sandy-giedeman/a/205/326

Read a Q&A about Sandra at Green Tara Press:

http://www.greentarapress.com/
author-interview-sandra-giedeman/